STOCKPORT
A Pictorial History

To Carol

With love and best

Wishes from

Roy

x x x

Map of East Cheshire, 1577.

STOCKPORT
A Pictorial History

Roy Westall

REWORD PUBLISHERS

1999

Published by
REWORD PUBLISHERS
3 Syddal Crescent
Bramhall
Cheshire SK7 1HS

Originally published
1988 by
Phillimore & Co. Ltd

ISBN 0 9536743 0 4

Printed and bound in Great Britain
by Biddles Ltd,
Guildford and King's Lynn

This book is dedicated to
My partner
Janet Maynard

List of Illustrations

Frontispiece: Map of East Cheshire, 1577

1. Map of Stockport, 1680
2. Stockport charter of 1220
3. Stockport charter of 1260
4. View of Stockport from Brinksway, 1793
5. Stockport from Brinksway Banks, 1876
6. The Plague Stone
7. Map of Stockport
8. St Mary's parish church, *c*.1800
9. St Mary's parish church
10. Chancel at the church
11. Interior view of the church
12. Figurehead on the chancel wall
13. The Old Rectory
14. The Folley
15. St Mary's parish church, *c*.1914
16. Stockport market place, 1810
17. The market place, 1859
18. The market place, 1896
19. Market scene
20. The Clog Shop
21. Advertisement for James Seal & Co.
22. Market traders in Victorian costume, 1985
23. Late 19th-century measures
24. Old houses on Rostron Brow, *c*.1880
25. Rostron Brow from the market place
26. The *Thatched Cottage* public house, Churchgate
27. Old Millgate, *c*.1890
28. St Mary's parish church, 1938
29. The Staircase Café
30. Rear of the Staircase Café
31. Drawing of the staircase, *c*.1880
32. Decaying upper room in the Staircase Café
33. Oak-panelled room
34. Medieval mullion window
35. Painting of Stockport, 1797
36. Stockport's medieval town wall
37. The castle yard, *c*.1886
38. The *County Hotel*
39. The *Bakers Vaults*
40. The *Angel Inn* and Market Hall, *c*.1880
41. Arched entrance to the Market House and the Free Library
42. Interior of the old Free Library
43. Winter's clock
44. Cobden's statue
45. St Peter's church and Cobden's statue
46. Clock in St Peter's church
47. St Peter's Square, *c*.1902
48. The Head Post Office in St Petersgate, *c*.1938.
49. Mansion House in Adlington Square
50. Girl and pram on Chestergate, *c*.1896
51. Chestergate and Adlington Square
52. Adlington Walk
53. Extract from Edward Shaa's will, 1487
54. Victorian impression of Edmund Shaa begging Richard III to take the crown
55. John Bradshaw's birth certificate
56. John Bradshaw
57. Charles I's death warrant
58. The Adlington family's town house, *c*.1880
59. The *Three Shires* wine bar
60. Union Street from Underbank
61. Vernon bridge and Union Street viewed from Princes Street, *c*.1937
62. Vernon Bridge and Union Street viewed from Underbank, *c*.1937
63. The old *White Lion*, 1901
64. The 'new' *White Lion*
65. Underbank Hall, *c*.1860
66. Underbank Hall, *c*.1880
67. Underbank Hall, now the National Westminster Bank
68. Entrance hall and staircase
69. Oak-framed wall
70. Stained-glass windows
71. Carved corbels
72. & 73. 17th-century fireplace
74. Grinling Gibbons fireplace
75. Detail from the fireplace
76. Thomas James Warren Bulkeley
77. Bridge Street
78. Bridge Street, *c*.1910
79. Bridge Street, *c*.1980
80. *Warren Bulkeley Arms Hotel* before demolition
81. *Warren Bulkeley Arms Hotel* during demolition
82. Lancashire Bridge, *c*.1930
83. The Mersey flowing under Lancashire Bridge
84. The flood stone
85. The *Buck and Dog*
86. Doorway of the *Buck and Dog Inn*
87. Tiviot Dale, *c*.1826
88. Tiviot Dale, *c*.1905
89. Pendlebury Hall viewed from Lancashire Hill
90. Pendlebury Hall
91. Tram in Princes Street
92. View of the Mersey
93. & 94. Construction of Merseyway, *c*.1939

95. View along Chestergate from Lower Carr Green, 1895
96. Sheep on Daw Bank
97. Mersey Square, c.1934
98. Traffic in Mersey Square
99. View of Mersey Square from Daw Bank, c.1920
100. Wellington Road South, c.1910
101. Map of Stockport and surrounding area, c.1800
102. Widening of the railway viaduct, 1887
103. Map of Stockport, 1824
104. Celebratory scene during widening of the viaduct, 1887
105. Scene on the viaduct, c.1888
106. Painting of Victorian Stockport
107. The Mersey and railway viaduct
108. The Mersey on its way to Liverpool
109. Stockport Mechanics' Institute, c.1880
110. Stockport Central Library
111. Stockport Town Hall viewed from the Art Gallery
112. Stockport Town Hall
113. Sir Brunwell Thomas
114. The Town Hall under construction
115. The Prince of Wales inspecting the Guard of Honour on Tiviot Dale Station Square, 7 July 1908
116. The Prince and Princess of Wales entering the Town Hall
117. Laying the Town Hall foundation stone, 15 October 1904
118. Placing of the top stone, 30 January 1907
119. First page of the visitors' book of Stockport Town Hall
120a. & b. Medal commemorating the opening of the Town Hall
121. Frontispiece of souvenir programme
122. Portrait of James Briscall
123. Grapes Steps Cottages, Middle Hillgate, 1910
124. Stockport Infirmary and the National Schools, c.1850 125. The Infirmary, c.1986
126. Mount Tabor chapel, c.1880
127. Stockport Grammar School, c.1888
128. Mount Tabor and the Technical College, c.1920
129. Oldest surviving record of Stockport Grammar School pupils, April 1837
130. Pupils of the Greek Street Grammar School
131. Robert John Brown, first headmaster of Stockport Technical School, c.1900
132. Syllabus for the Technical School, 1897
133. The boys' class, 1891
134. The girls' class, 1891
135. The teachers, c.1891

136. The spinning room, c.1897
137. The carpentry class, c.1897
138. The chemistry laboratory, c.1897
139. Students being given a chemistry lesson, c.1897
140. Stockport Technical School, c.1890
141. Technical School being used as a hospital, 1917
142. St Thomas's church
143. Mule and steam power, Middle Hillgate
144. Corner of Edward Street and Middle Hillgate
145. Bricklayers, c.1895
146. Christy & Co., 1937
147. Mr. Boardman finishing a bowler in Christy's
148. Stockport from Reddish, 1810
149. Stockport from Reddish, 1885
150. Samuel Oldknow's house
151. Mule spinning, 1910
152. Flax drying on Turncroft Lane, c.1920
153. Constable Birch's breastbone
154. The memoirs of Jacob McGhinness
155. The *Bishop Blaize* public house, c.1852
156. The *Gladstone*
157. Rioters attacking chapel at Edgeley, c.1852
158. The attack on St Peter's Schools and Alderman Graham's house, c.1852
159. Crowther Street in 1930 by L. S. Lowry
160. Crowther Street as it appears today
161. L. S. Lowry sketching Stockport Viaduct
162. Dam on Higher Carr, Waterloo Road
163. Junction of Lower Hillgate, High Street and Wellington Street, 1907
164. The same view today
165. Frederic and Emma Robinson
166. Robinson's Brewery, Hillgate, 1913
167. Robinson's Brewery, May 1937
168. Delivery vehicles from F. Robinson & Co., 1922
169. Coopers at work in Robinson's Brewery
170. Robinson's dray horses in the market place
171. Rostron Brow
172. Lower Hillgate, c.1910
173. Lower Hillgate
174. Business card of Messrs. Kay Bros.
175. Advertisement for Cragg & Walker
176. Junction of Little Underbank and Mealhouse Brow
177. Jonathan Thatcher riding into Stockport, c.1784
178. Constable's leather helmet, c.1820
179. An 1880 drawing of the scold's bridle
180. Facsimile of the first issue of the *Stockport Advertiser*
181-4. Four billposters for Stockport theatres

Acknowledgements

I wish to express my gratitude to the following people and organisations for allowing me to reproduce photographs which they own: Crispin Eurich, no. 161; The First Gallery, Southampton, no. 161; Frederic Robinson Ltd., nos. 165, 166, 167; Stockport Central Library, nos. 15, 18, 28, 37, 40, 47, 50, 51, 78, 88, 92, 95, 96, 97, 100, 102, 104, 105, 107, 112, 123, 144, 151, 163, 168, 172; Stockport College of Technology, nos. 63, 77, 99, 131, 132, 133, 134, 135, 136, 137, 138, 139, 140, 141; *Stockport Express Advertiser & Times*; Stockport Grammar School, nos. 36, 49, 53, 54, 128, 129, 130; Stockport Museum, nos. 6, 23, 147, 153, 154, 169, 178.

I would also like to thank Father Kenrick for allowing me to take photographs inside St Peter's church, and the National Westminster Bank for allowing me to take photographs inside Underbank Hall.

Finally, my special thanks to Beryl Baguley, not only for allowing me to reproduce some of her excellent drawings of Stockport (nos. 19, 45, 59), but also for the time and effort that she put into preparing the map (no. 7) specially for this book.

Stockport boasts its springs and fountains
 Many streets as steep as mountains,
Rosy cheeks and bright-eyed lasses,
 Youths which toast them in their glasses,
Church and castle, tower and steeple,
 And a loyal, happy people.

Barnaby's Journal

Introduction

As the glaciers retreated in the wake of the Ice Age, a drier and warmer climate followed and the greater part of Cheshire became dominated by vast oak woodlands. In the foothills of the Pennines, however, birch and peaty boglands were predominant. In the area surrounding Stockport, several Stone and Bronze Age axes have been discovered.

Although no Roman relics have been found in the town, there is little doubt that Stockport, situated on a steep elevation above the River Mersey, was an outpost or camp for the Roman garrison in Manchester. The Manchester to Buxton Roman road would certainly have passed through the town.

Saxon crosses have been found in Cheadle, Disley, Bollington Bow-Stones, Prestbury, Rainow and Macclesfield and are an ever-present reminder of the Christian faith of our forefathers. Even the name Stockport is of Saxon origin, meaning 'fortified or stockaded place in the woods'.

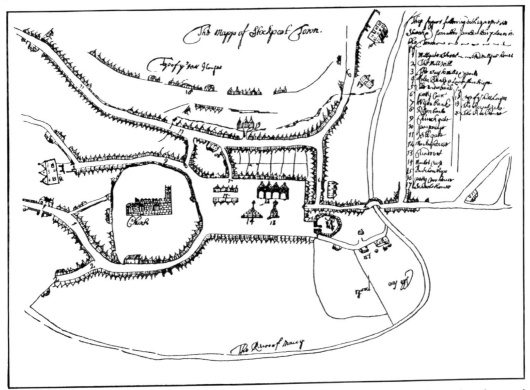

1. Map of Stockport, 1680. This ancient map shows the parish church and rectory, the market place and 'castle', as well as the River Mersey and Lancashire Bridge.

2. Stockport charter of 1220 which made the borough a free town.

3. Charter of 1260 allowing the town to hold a weekly market and annual fair.

4. View of Stockport from Brinksway in 1793.

5. Stockport from Brinksway Banks in 1876.

During this period, Stockport obviously declined as a town since there is no mention of it in the Domesday Book. Bramhall and Norbury were meeting similar fates. At the time of Edward the Confessor they were worth 32 shillings and 10 shillings respectively; by 1086, however, they were worth only five shillings and three shillings. One of the earliest mentions of the town is in a 12th-century charter in which Baron de Stokeport exchanged a plot of land, its buildings and a little garden enclosed by an old ditch on the banks of the Mersey, together with any driftwood from the river, for land in Romiley. At this time, Stockport was part of Macclesfield forest and it was, of course, the profusion of trees in the area that made Cheshire famous for its timber-framed houses.

However, the town's most important charters were those of c.1220, in which Sir Robert de Stokeport made the town a free borough, and 1260, when the lord of the manor received the right to hold a market every Friday, as well as an annual fair on St Wilfrid's Day (12 October) and the following seven days. This right was a closely guarded privilege, since he would receive the income from the market tolls. Stockport's medieval market would have presented a colourful and varied scene, with traders selling corn and flour, cattle, sheep, goats and pigs, as well as fleeces, hides and skins. Salt would have been an important commodity, as would utensils made from copper, iron and lead, mined at nearby Alderley Edge.

By the 17th century, the manor had grown extensively and William Webb, writing in 1614, describes it thus:

6. The Plague Stone. In 1605-6 many Stopfordians died of the plague. In order to stop the spread of the disease, traders would exchange money by placing it in vinegar contained in this stone trough.

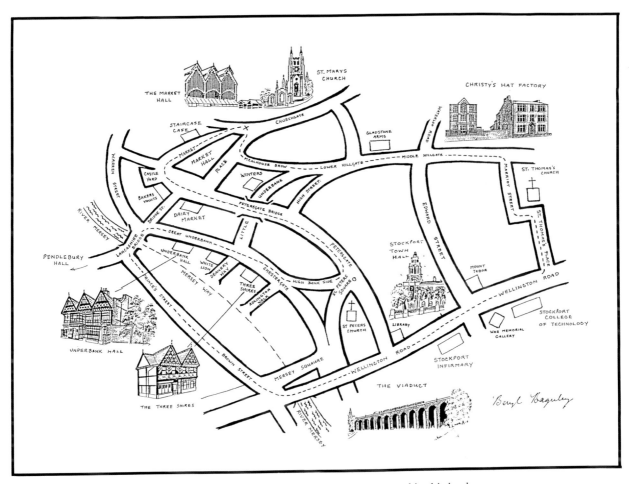

7. A map of Stockport showing the areas covered in this book.

Upon one round Hill hath this town of Stockport been built, the summity or top whereof affords the Market-place and convenient room for the church; and for the Parsonage, which are very fair ones, the right of presentation belonging to the Worshipful house of POYNTON, the skirt of the Hill beautified by many fair Buildings and half about the skirt of it runs the MERSEY, with great force or rather fury under a great stone-bridge, which divides them from Lancashire; it is a great market, and much frequented by dwellers far remote.

The Market Place

St Mary's parish church

For almost 700 years bells have rung out from this elevated site, calling on its parishioners from as far away as Hyde, Werneth and Disley to come to worship. By the 19th century, however, the soft sandstone tower had become unsafe, probably due to erosion; some believed it was a possible result of the continuous ringing of the bells to celebrate Nelson's victory at Trafalgar. Even so, its demolition required the aid of battering rams and gunpowder. Fortunately, the 14th-century chancel, clergy vestry and oratory were saved and a new tower and nave were added between 1813 and 1817, with further modifications in 1848 and 1882. The tower itself is 95 ft. high, surmounted by 30 ft. pinnacles. This combination of 14th- and 19th-century building styles produces a unique but pleasing church of which all Stopfordians may be proud.

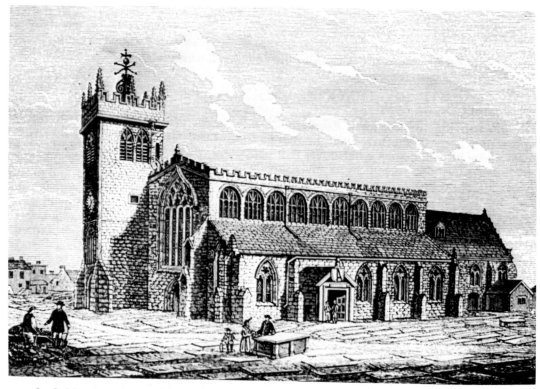

8. St Mary's parish church c.1800, before its demolition. The weathercock now stands on Disley parish church.

9. St Mary's parish church as it now appears.

10. The 14th-century chancel of St Mary's parish church.

11. (*above*) Inside St Mary's parish church.

12. (*above*) A carved stone figurehead on the chancel wall.

14. (*below*) The Folley. At the end of this narrow passageway behind St Mary's church stood almshouses, bequeathed in 1684 by Edward Warren of Poynton.

13. (*below*) The Old Rectory. This delightful Georgian house, on a hill overlooking the church, occupies the site of an older rectory, as can be seen in the map of 1680 (*see* plate 1).

The Market Place

This square has been in use since 1260 when the lord of the manor received a charter granting him the right to hold a weekly market and annual fair. In Elizabethan times, two rows of shops stood in the market place, on the right a cheese house and on the left a market house and butchers' shambles. These were demolished in 1824 to allow the market area to be extended.

In the centre was a market cross raised on six steps. From here banns of marriage were proclaimed on three consecutive market days. The building that now dominates this area is the elegant and recently restored Victorian indoor market. Built in 1861 from iron and glass, its design was influenced by the Great Exhibition's Crystal Palace, constructed 10 years earlier.

15. St Mary's parish church, *c.*1914. The Staircase Café can be seen on the left.

16. Stockport market place in 1810.

17. The market place in 1859, shortly before the building of the indoor market. The mealhouse and butchers' shambles have been demolished.

18. A view of the market place, *c*.1896. Notice James Seal's tobacco factory on the left.

19. The hustle and bustle of the market.

THE MARKET PLACE, STOCKPORT

20. The Clog Shop. This traditional craft shop was opened in the 1950s. The premises were once part of James Seal's factory.

21. An advertisement for James Seal & Co., tobacco manufacturers.

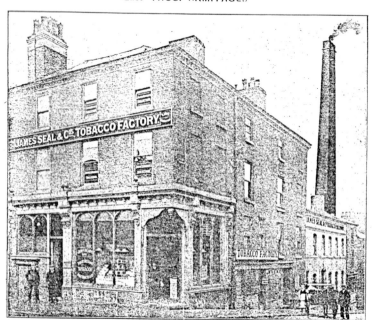

Factories: MARKET PLACE and PARK STREET, Stockport

JAMES SEAL & CO.
(Late THOS. ARMITAGE.)

Manufacturers of every description of
Spun and Cut Tobaccos.

RICHMOND FLAKE

✵

BROWN VIRGINIA FLAKE.

✵

BLACK FLAKE.

✵

HONEY DEW FLAKE.

✵

SMOKE SEAL'S "COLDEN OCTAVE" CIGARETTES.

Established 1860.

"COLDEN" NAVY CUT.

✵

"LILY," "EMPRESS," AND "CROWN" MIXTURES.

✵

"JOLLY TAR" AND "STOCKPORT." CHESTER CUT.

✵

SMOKE SEAL'S "OCTAVE" WHIFFS.

Cigars of the Finest Brands.   All kinds of Cigarettes kept in Stock.

22. Market traders dressed in Victorian costume in September 1985 to celebrate the restoration of Stockport's magnificent Market Hall.

23. These measures, dating from the late 19th century, were used by the market inspector to ensure traders were selling the full quantity of goods.

24. Old houses on Rostron Brow, *c.*1880.

25. Rostron Brow from the market place. The building on the right has been demolished.

26.   The *Thatched Cottage* public house on Churchgate. It was at the ancient hostelry of the same name that James Briscall opened his consulting room.

27.   Old Millgate, *c.*1890. On the right is the *Arden Arms* public house which still stands today. A car salesroom now occupies the site of the thatched cottage.

28. St Mary's parish church in 1938. Wilde's shoe shop, now the Staircase Café, can be seen on the left. This name is still laid out in mosaic in the doorway of the building.

The Staircase Café

In the middle of a row of shops stands the Staircase Café. From its rather drab brick frontage one may be forgiven for giving it little more than a cursory glance. However, a closer inspection of the rear of the building will reveal part of the superb timber framing and wattle and daub infill. Dating from the latter part of the 15th century, this cruck-framed shop gets its name from the intricately carved Jacobean 'cage newel' staircase, now hidden from the public gaze.

The building contains a labyrinth of 17th- and 18th-century oak-panelled rooms, whilst the cellars and sub-cellars appear to be medieval. It has been suggested that the large sandstone blocks which make up part of these cellars were originally part of either the town wall or the castle. In the 19th century the building was owned by the Wild family, who conducted their boot and shoe business from the premises; their name can still be seen in the mosaic floor in the doorway. Mr. W. I. Wild was president of the literary society and many meetings were held here.

29. The building next door to A. J. Gleave is the Staircase Café. The brick facade hides a 15th-century cruck-framed town house.

30. Rear of the Staircase Café showing timber-framing and one of the medieval vaulted cellars.

31. A drawing of the staircase, *c.*1880.

32. A decaying upper room in the Staircase Café. The fire-place is dated 1688.

33. Oak-panelled room.

34. Medieval mullion window in one of the cellars.

Stockport Castle

On the north side of the market place stands an open area known as Castle Yard. When the Romans built a road between Manchester and Buxton, a ford was necessary to cross the River Mersey. This was situated at nearby Tiviot Dale. It is believed that around A.D. 79 they fortified a hillock on the south side of the river to overlook the crossing. A castle was later constructed by the Normans and in 1172 was held by Geoffrey de Costentyn, a son of Henry II, in a rebellion against his father. It is unlikely that the castle existed beyond the 14th century, although later records refer to castle hill.

In 1775 Sir George Warren, as lord of the manor, had the yard levelled and a circular brick turret built on the site. This was subsequently demolished by a later lord of the manor and in 1853 the area was lowered so that it could be used as a cattle market.

35. A 1797 painting of Stockport showing the Old Rectory, St Mary's parish church and the brick 'castle'.

36. A recent photograph of part of Stockport's medieval town wall. Note the buttress and gargoyle.

37. The castle yard *c.*1886, after it had been lowered for use as a cattle market.

38. The *County Hotel*, now demolished, which stood near the Castle Yard.

The *Bakers Vaults*

Near the Castle Yard is the *Bakers Vaults* public house. First mentioned in 1821, this inn was originally the *George and Dragon* and was run by the Baker family. In 1841 it was demolished when the market place was enlarged and the new public house built on the site became known as the *Bakers Vaults*. The town stocks, where minor offenders would be fastened for a few hours, originally stood by the parish church. However, as this annoyed the worshippers, they were moved first to the top of Mealhouse Brow and later near to the *Bakers Vaults*.

39. The *Bakers Vaults*, at the top of Bridge Street Brow.

Market House and Library

Near the *Bakers Vaults* is the impressive arched entrance to the old market house. Twenty years after the demolition of the cheese house and butchers' shambles in the market square, it became evident that alternative premises were needed. On the chosen site stood an ancient half-timbered building which, prior to the opening of new premises in St Petersgate on 14 October 1836, had served as the town's post office. At this time charges were made according to distance carried and a single sheet letter to London cost 11d. (4½p) and a letter containing two sheets cost 22d. (9p). Horse-drawn coaches travelling to all parts of the country would stop at the post office to collect the mail.

The old building was demolished, the foundation stone for the cheese market was laid on 17 September 1851 and the building was opened on 28 April of the following year. For over 130 years the inhabitants of Stockport have come to this hall to purchase delicious local produce: traditional cheeses, bacon, eggs, sausages, black puddings and pies.

In 1853 the Council of Stockport appointed a committee to examine the desirability of establishing a free library in the town. After recommending a postponement in the belief that the Mechanics' Institution met the current need, little was done until 19 years later when a second committee supported the venture. The market house was altered by the addition of an upper floor, fronted by the magnificent portico. The Stockport Free Library opened on 20 September 1875 with a stock of 5,994 volumes.

40. The *Angel Inn* and Market Hall, *c*.1880. The *Angel Inn* dates from *c*.1820 and was closed on 29 September 1951. The site is now occupied by Cheshire Building Society.

41. (*left*) The arched entrance to the Market House (opened in 1852) and, above it, the first Free Library (opened in 1875).

42. (*above*) Interior of the old Free Library.

St Petersgate

St Petersgate Bridge

Designed by C. Rawlinson and built at a cost of £10,500, St Petersgate Bridge has always been a delight to the town. Prior to its public opening on 24 February 1868, the only way to cross from the market square to St Petersgate was via steep steps or brows into the Underbanks. The bridge did not please everybody, however, the shopkeepers of Underbank fearing that they would lose business.

Winter's Clock

Around 1880 Jacob Winter moved to Little Underbank from Hillgate. He originally owned one jewellery shop and then later extended into neighbouring premises. On early closing day he would travel to Alderley and Wilmslow by pony and trap to collect watches and clocks for repair.

   His shop is notable for its clock, whose three figures strike bells every 15 minutes. The building is extraordinarily secure for, like many of the shops in this part of Stockport, Winter's is built into the rockface and does not have a rear exit. Although it is no longer in use, Jacob Winter installed a unique security device into one of his shop windows. Hydraulically operated by natural spring water, the entire window and contents can be lowered into the shop cellar.

43. Winter's clock.

Richard Cobden (1804-1865)

Richard Cobden was born on 3 June 1804 at Dunford, near Midhurst in Sussex, the son of a poor farmer. The family was large, Richard being the fourth of eleven children and, although fortunate in being sent by his uncle to a school in Yorkshire, he described his education as being a 'mockery'.

At the age of 15 he obtained a clerical position at a warehouse in London. Three years later, having found the job unpleasant, he accepted an offer from a business house in Ghent. He made such a good impression that at the age of 21 he was promoted to commercial traveller. However, his ambitions were cut short when, in 1826, the company went bankrupt. Two years later he heard that a company named Fort & Co. were about to close a calico print works at Sabden in Lancashire. Travelling with two colleagues on 'The Peveril of the Peak' coach, a journey which from London would take over 20 hours, he was able to persuade Messrs. Fort not only to let him take over the mill and produce prints on a commission basis, but for them to provide capital as well. Finding accommodation at 6 Mosley Street, Manchester, Cobden earnestly set to work and within a few years 'Cobden prints' were very much in demand and fetched high prices.

Richard Cobden's involvement in the Lancashire community awakened a political interest. He cared for the working class, aiding his employees with cheap goods and improving their education by opening a library in Sabden. He believed the best way of improving the lot of the poor was by the abolition of the Corn Laws. These imposed high levels of taxation on all imported corn with the result that the tenant farmers made vast profits from locally-grown grain, the landed gentry were able to demand high rents and the working classes lived on the verge of starvation, unable to afford the expensive bread.

In 1838 Cobden was one of seven men who gathered in a little room over the stables of the *York Hotel* in Manchester, and took the first steps towards the formation of the Anti-Corn Law League. This pressure group was never short of money as it was backed by the entire cotton interests of Lancashire, eager for cheaper raw material and enlarged markets for their finished goods. Possessing outstanding powers of oratory, Cobden was described as having 'a blend of extraordinary persuasiveness of appeal, fiery energy, ardour for the tactics of battle, and with a passion of sincerity'.

In 1841 Cobden was elected to represent Stockport in the House of Commons, a position he held for six years. In July 1847, although re-elected virtually unopposed in Stockport, he also won the seat for the West Riding of Yorkshire, then the largest constituency in the country. With apparent regret, he took up the latter seat.

By today's standards, Richard Cobden's views would appear to be a conundrum of liberal thinking. Fighting for free trade, he described those who defended the protection of agricultural prices as 'monopolists', and believed that Britain should loosen its ties with the colonies. However, he also opposed trade unionism and fought bitterly against attempts to introduce legislation to control the use of child labour. Despite this, Richard Cobden was well liked and his death on 2 April 1865 was met with profound sorrow throughout the nation. He was buried at Lavington, Midhurst, at the side of his son, the funeral being attended by the Mayor of Stockport.

Cobden's statue in St Petersgate appears to be the only statue in the town. Made from bronze by George C. Adams, F.S.A., of London, the figure is 8 ft. high and stands on a square bronze base surmounted upon a block of Aberdeen granite 10 ft. high and weighing 10 tons. It was unveiled on 27 November 1886 by his third daughter, Jane Cobden. The ceremony was attended by such a multitude of people that the proceedings were hurried to save the discomfort of the crowd.

44. Cobden's statue.

45. St Peter's church and Cobden's statue.

St. Peter's Church, Stockport.
CONSECRATED A.D. 1768

St Peter's church

Until the middle of the 18th century, St Mary's parish church was the only place of worship in Stockport. As the town began to grow, the need for greater accommodation, particularly for those coming from the west of the town, became evident. William Wright, a former mayor of Stockport whose town residence was Mansion House, Top o' the Hill (High Street), paid for the construction of the church, sited amongst fields and gardens. This necessitated the improvement of a footpath which, at that time, was the only means of reaching the church from High Street.

St Peter's was consecrated on 31 May 1768 by Bishop Keene of Chester and originally seated 458 people, pews at that time being rented. In 1838 the church's seating capacity was increased by the construction of north and south galleries but these were removed 50 years later during the building of the chancel. On 19 June 1768, Mary Wolstencroft, a spinster of Stockport, became the first person to be interred. Her gravestone read:

> Within these sacred walls the first am I,
> Whom providence ordained here to lie
> A spotless saint, tho' now consign'd to dust
> To wait the resurrection of the just.

The majority of the fittings in the church are 20th-century, with one particular exception – the chair-frame clock which stands in the entrance. Made by John Whitehurst, this most unusual mechanism was installed in the tower in 1769, the year after the church was built, and is reputed to be the oldest public clock in Greater Manchester. At the turn of this century the clock fell into disrepair and was removed from the tower. Recently restored, it is planned to return it to its former place once desperately-needed funds are obtained.

46. The clock in St Peter's church – the oldest public clock in Greater Manchester.

47. St Peter's Square, *c.*1902. The building in the centre is the Theatre Royal Opera House. Opened on 4 June 1888, many music hall stars appeared here including Gracie Fields and Charlie Chaplin. The theatre was demolished in 1962.

48. The Head Post Office in St Petersgate, *c.*1938. The building is now occupied by the R.A.C

Chestergate

Adlington Square

It is difficult to imagine that an ancient square once stood in this area which now contains only the post office, the entrance into Merseyway shopping precinct, several shops and a few steps and seats. Only two clues give any indication of its former glory, the first being the name Adlington Walk. Previously known as Adlington Square, the area once belonged to the Leghs of Adlington and contained early 17th-century brick buildings. A century later, the square consisted almost entirely of grand residences set amongst gardens and fields.

At about this time, 'the Mansion House' was constructed by the Leghs. A large house, it was described as having a wide hall, noble staircase and lofty rooms. The gardens extended to the river which could be reached by steps down the rock face, a spot which was particularly good for fishing. Later, the house was sold to John Dale (mayor in 1775) who built a water-powered weaving and spinning mill in the square. Industry had arrived.

The second clue to the area's past is the brass plate which states: 'Here stood Stockport Grammar School/1607-1832/Founded by Sir Edmund Shaa/A.D. 1487'.

49. A rare photograph of the Mansion House in Adlington Square.

50. This charming photograph was taken on Chestergate around 1896, near the present Halifax Building Society. Notice how narrow the road is.

51.   Chestergate and Adlington Square. The photograph shows, from left to right: C.W.S. Travel Agent, Prescott's, Oddfellows' Hall, the *Bull and Coppock*, Blackham's, Adlington Square and Kelsall's.

52.   Adlington Walk. Stockport Grammar School once stood here.

Stockport Grammar School

Edmund Shaa, a native of Stockport, was apprenticed to a jeweller in London. Highly successful, he later became a member of the Goldsmiths Company, then Mayor of London and ultimately Jeweller to Kings Edward IV, Richard III and Henry VII. When he died in 1487 he left a will in which a small amount of money was to be invested by the Goldsmiths Company, the income from which was to be used for a free Grammar School. He specified that education there should be made available to any of the boys of Stockport and the neighbouring towns who wished to attend. In addition, £10 p.a. was to be paid to the schoolmaster.

The bequest was used to purchase land and houses in central London. Although this brought in a high income, it appears to have been used more for the enrichment of the Goldsmiths Company than for the people of Stockport, for until 1829 the company continued to pay the schoolmaster only the £10 specified centuries earlier.

From the 17th century the school was housed in a small two-storey building in the Square. In earlier times lessons had been given in St Mary's parish church. Due to the encroachment of industry in this part of Stockport, a plot of land on the corner of Greek Street and Wellington Road South was obtained from Lady Vernon for the site of a new school. Opened amidst great ceremony on 30 April 1832, it was known as the Stockport Grammar and Free School. As well as the school building, there were also residences for the masters. In 1916 the school was moved once more to Mile End Lane, Davenport, as increased traffic had made teaching difficult. The Greek Street site is now occupied by the War Memorial and Art Gallery.

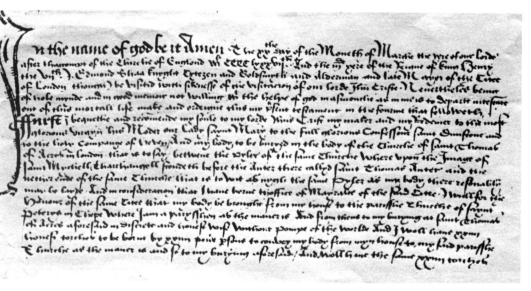

53. An extract from Edmund Shaa's will, 1487.

OFFER OF THE KINGSHIP TO RICHARD DUKE OF GLOUCESTER AT BAYNARD'S CASTLE JUNE 26TH 1483

54. A Victorian impression of Edmund Shaa begging Richard III to take the crown. This painting hangs in the Goldsmith's Hall in London.

John Bradshaw (1602-59)

Born at Wibersley Hall, situated between High Lane and Disley, John Bradshaw was the second surviving son of Henry Bradshaw, a wealthy country gentleman of Marple Hall, and Catherine, daughter of Ralph Winnington of Offerton Hall. The records of St Mary's church show that on 10 December 1602 John Bradshaw was baptised here. Following the entry, the word 'Traitor' has been added. Educated first at Stockport's Free School and later at Bunbury in Cheshire, he was able to obtain a position as clerk to an attorney at Congleton, thereby gaining a shrewd knowledge of the law. He continued to study law in London and on 23 April 1627 was called to the bar at Gray's Inn. In 1630 he was appointed Steward of the Manor of Glossop and in 1637 Mayor of Congleton. He was later to become High Steward of this borough.

By this time he had become a highly influential and renowned lawyer, siding with the Parliamentarians who opposed many of the monarch's 'tyrannical' powers. In June 1647 he was a member of the council retained for the prosecution of the royalist Judge Jenkins on the charge of passing judgement of death on men who had fought for Parliament during the Civil War. On 3 January 1649, the House of Commons appointed a Court of Commissioners to proceed with the trial of Charles I. Five days later, John Bradshaw was made president of this court (some say with reluctance). After several preliminary meetings, the trial began on 20 January at Westminster Hall. Dressed in black and seated on a crimson chair, surrounded by 80 members of the court, Bradshaw must have been an awesome sight for the king when he appeared before him. The trial continued for several weeks, the king refusing to acknowledge the jurisdiction of the court. On 27 January the court met for the last time, with Bradshaw and his fellow commissioners surrounded by an armed guard. The drama of the scene is recorded by Lord Clarendon in his *History of the Rebellion* (1707):

> Silence having been demanded, the Lord President proceeded to deliver a long and bitter address in justification of the Court, about to be read aloud, during which the King made many attempts to obtain permission to speak, but was not permitted, as he had frequently refused to acknowledge the authority of the Court. The President thus concluded: 'It is our part and duties to do what the Law prescribes. We are not here to give Law but to say what is the Law. We cannot be unmindful of what the Scripture tells us, for to acquit the guilty is an equal abomination as to condemn the innocent. We may not acquit the guilty. What sentence the Law affirms to a traitor, tyrant, a murderer, and a publick enemy to the Country, that sentence you are now to hear read unto you; and that is the sentence of the Court.'

The sentence of execution was carried out the following day. John Bradshaw was rewarded by being given the highest office in the kingdom – President of the Council of State.

Following a long illness, Bradshaw died on 31 October 1659 and was buried with great pomp and ceremony in Westminster Abbey on 22 November.

55. John Bradshaw's birth certificate.

56. John Bradshaw.

57. Charles I's death warrant. The first signature (on the left) is that of John Bradshaw, followed by Thomas Grey and then Oliver Cromwell.

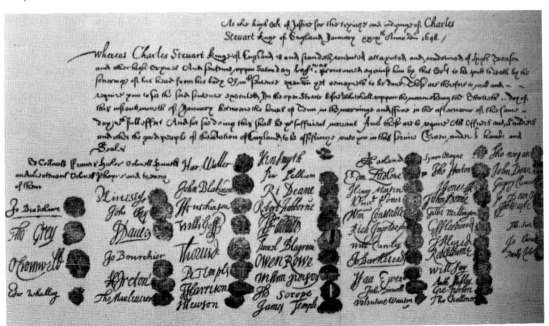

The *Three Shires Wine Bar*

Near the post office stands one of Stockport's most cherished buildings, the premises of Smith, Fort and Symond's (solicitors) and the *Three Shires Wine Bar*. This timber-framed structure was once the town residence of the Leghs of Adlington, although by the 18th century it was owned by the Tattons. The exact age of the building is not known but the earliest deeds are dated 19 September 1657.

58. A drawing (*c.*1880) of the Adlington family's town house, now the *Three Shires* wine bar.

59. A drawing of the *Three Shires* wine bar.

Deanery Way
(formerly Union Road)

At the junction of the Underbanks is Deanery Way, a narrow thoroughfare leading into the Merseyway precinct and beyond to Princes Street. Before the covering of the Mersey in the 1960s, the Lancashire and Cheshire sides of the street were connected by an iron footbridge, built in 1875 at a cost of £650.

The first bridge to cross the river at this point was made of wood and opened in 1828, using land given by the Philanthropic Society. An inn known as the *Union Tavern* was constructed at the same time. The crossing was replaced in 1858 and again in 1870. Five years later it was dismantled to make way for the iron Vernon Bridge.

60. Union Street from Underbank.

61. Vernon Bridge and Union Street viewed from Princes Street, *c*.1937.

62. Vernon Bridge and Union Street viewed from Underbank, *c*.1937.

The *White Lion*

On the corner of Great Underbank and Deanery Way stands the *White Lion Inn*. Built earlier this century, it occupies the site of an ancient black and white timber-framed inn of the same name. Roads to the east, south and west meet here and as a consequence this place became the most important posting house and hotel in the town.

The hostelry had its own brew house and stables, a bowling green, as well as rights to fish for salmon in the river which ran at the bottom of its garden. Public coaches called here every day for passengers and parcels. The gentry held banquets here, and on market days farmers gathered to fix prices for their wares. It is said that on 25 March 1831 William Clayton fastened a halter around his wife's neck and sold her here to J. Booth for five shillings. As with most villages and towns, local business revolved around church and inn. The town crier stood outside the *White Lion* to announce the latest news, and during the Peninsula Wars a cannon, always kept loaded in the stables, was fired to let the people of Stockport know of the arrival of the mailcoach.

It is interesting to note that pub lunches are not a modern invention, for it is recorded that in 1758 the mayor held a banquet at the *White Lion*, the bill amounting to:

	£	s.	d.
76 Dinners at one shilling per head	3	16	-
Wine, Punch, Ale and Porter	5	14	3
Music 10s., Singers 6s., Ringers 3s.	-	19	-
Huntsman & Keeper 1s., Servants 6s.	-	7	-
Two bottles of wine from White Lion	-	4	-
Four bottles of wine from Bulls Head	-	6	8
Expences at John Booth's	-	10	-
Gloves for self and Bailiff	-	2	6
Expences at Bull's Head	-	2	10
Paid Mr. William Cooper for speech	-	5	-
	12	7	3

63. The old *White Lion* in 1901, decorated in celebration of the coronation of Edward VII.

64. A view of the 'new' *White Lion*, standing at the junction of Union Street, Underbank, Little Underbank and Chestergate.

Underbank Hall

The walk along Great Underbank leads to Stockport's most historic house – Underbank Hall. Although the walk covers only a few yards, this distance was particularly difficult to negotiate in the late 18th century, Underbank being very narrow and spanned by an archway between the *White Lion* and Underbank Hall. This arch was one of several in Stockport, erected to close the town off in times of danger. In order to pass through, it was necessary for carts and waggons to reduce their loads. Beautifully preserved by the National Westminster Bank, the hall is characterised by the half-timbered façade which was once so typical of Cheshire houses. Its age is unknown, but it is thought to be late 15th- or early 16th-century and was built as the town house of the Ardernes of Harden, whose country residence was in Bredbury. William Shakespeare's mother was a descendant of the Warwickshire branch of this same family.

The hall remained with the Ardernes until 1823 when it was sold by Lord Alvaney for 3,000 guineas, the buyers being Messrs. John Winterbottom, William Christy, Isaac Lloyd and John Worsley, who required it for banking purposes. Unsuccessful attempts were made by the Court Leet to buy the house for use as a town hall. Later it was sold to the Manchester and Liverpool District Banking Company and has remained in use as a bank ever since.

The front of the building contains two oak-panelled rooms, a staircase and entrance hall, all of which have seen very little alteration. On entering the banking hall, one is immediately struck by the size. The hammer-beamed roof has majestically carved corbels, each one a different design. Surprisingly, this hall was built in 1915, replacing 18th-century brick extensions, themselves constructed on the site of the gardens, which extended to the river. Also in the banking hall is a large and ancient fireplace. This was brought here in 1623 as part of the dowry of Eleanor, daughter of Sir John Done of Utkington Hall near Tarporley, who married Ralph Arderne in the same year. There is also another finely carved fireplace in the manager's office, believed to be the work of Grinling Gibbons.

65.   A drawing of Underbank Hall, *c*.1860.

66. A drawing of Underbank Hall, c.1880.

67. A recent photograph of Underbank Hall, now owned by the National Westminster Bank.

68. Entrance hall and staircase, Underbank Hall.

69. An oak-framed wall in Underbank Hall.

70. Stained-glass windows in one of the upper rooms at Underbank Hall.

71. Carved corbels in Underbank Hall.

72. & 73. The magnificent 17th-century fireplace in
Underbank Hall, part of the dowry of Eleanor Done of
Utkington. The drawing was made in about 1880.

74.   The Grinling Gibbons fireplace.

75.   Detail from the Grinling Gibbons fireplace.

The *Warren Bulkeley*

During the construction of Warren Street in 1785, an ancient hostelry known as the *Anchor Inn* was pulled down and the *Warren Bulkeley Inn* was built on the site. Named after the lord of the manor, it was sumptuously appointed and became a much favoured meeting house. It was here on 23 March 1824 that the decision was made to build Wellington Road. Unfortunately, the *Warren Bulkeley* has recently met the same fate as the *Anchor Inn* although its frontage, originally in Bridge Street, is currently being re-erected in Warren Street.

76. Thomas James Warren Bulkeley, Lord of the Manor of Stockport.

77. An old photograph of Bridge Street, showing the *Buck and Dog* (left) and the *Warren Bulkeley* (centre).

78. A view of Bridge Street, c.1910.

79. A view of Bridge Street, c.1980.

80. Bridge Street showing the *Warren Bulkeley Arms Hotel* before demolition.

81. The *Warren Bulkeley Arms Hotel* during demolition.

The Mersey

Prior to the 1974 boundary changes, Lancashire Bridge, the oldest crossing point of the Mersey in the town, linked Cheshire with Lancashire; the polluted water of the river flows beneath it before disappearing under the Merseyway shopping precinct, re-emerging at the far side of Mersey Square.

The river has not always been so polluted. In October 1655 John Cheetham was fined for killing salmon out of season and in 1822 an anonymous poet wrote:

> On Turncroft's rough romantic steep
>   Wrapt with the scene oft have I stood
> To watch the gurgling crystal sweep
>   Along a ceaseless winding flood.
> I'm pleased by thee thou lovely stream,
>   At morn, or eve, to walk alone
> And look upon thy face and dream
>   Of venerable ages gone.

The Mersey is formed by the confluence of three other rivers: the Tame, Goyt and Etherow. The exact source of the Mersey is the subject of much debate, the favourite theory being that it rises as a spring in Woodhead, where Yorkshire, Lancashire and Cheshire meet, and flows to join the Goyt near Mottram. The Tame flows from Micklehurst in Yorkshire and down a valley through Stalybridge, Ashton, Hyde, Denton and Reddish, forming the boundary between Lancashire and Cheshire. It joins the Mersey a few hundred yards upstream from Lancashire Bridge.

The Roman road from Manchester to Buxton would have taken a route through Longsight and along Old Road (Heaton Norris) to Tiviot Dale, crossing a ford on the river about 200 yards above Lancashire Bridge.

It is recorded that in the 14th century there was a little chapel or hermitage on the bridge. Here, a hermit took up his abode and, on payment of a small coin, would offer up prayers for the safety of the wayfarer. Since then, the bridge has been replaced many times. In November 1745 it was blown up to prevent the army of Charles Stuart, the Young Pretender, from advancing into Cheshire, having already reached Manchester. In 1805 the bridge was described as being 'founded on a red rock with one arch allowed to be the largest in the kingdom'. In recent years the flow of the river has been tamed by the construction of weirs and dams upstream. However, an indication of its previous ferocity is given by the words inscribed on a stone, embedded in the right-hand wall of the recently demolished *Buck and Dog Inn*: '17th of August 1799 this River was as high as the top of this stone. James Brown.'. The stone was over 20 ft. above the present river level.

82. Lancashire Bridge during the construction of Merseyway, *c.*1930.

83. The Mersey flowing under Lancashire Bridge. Warren Street and Bridge Street can be seen in the background and the *Buck and Dog* is on the right. New development on the bridge has hidden this view.

The *Buck and Dog Inn*

James Brown was the owner of the *Buck and Dog* from about 1770. Situated at a principal crossing into Stockport, this inn was an important posting station. During the Napoleonic wars the hostelry was used for military purposes and many disturbances occurred when locals were press-ganged into service. The place fell into disrepute and the owner was ultimately obliged to sell his house to Messrs. Hole and Harrison, the predecessors of Boddington's Brewery. In 1815 and for a further 30 years, the *Buck and Dog* was run by Ellis Shawcross, who was able to restore its good reputation.

84. The flood stone, built into the *Buck and Dog*.

85. The *Buck and Dog* before demolition.

86. The doorway of the *Buck and Dog Inn*.

Pendlebury Hall

The red brick and stone building towering high over Lancashire Hill is Pendlebury Hall. Built as an orphanage from a £100,000 bequest from Sir Ralph Pendlebury J.P. (1790-1861), the hall was opened on 20 April 1882. The dormitories were large in size but small in number, the founder stipulating that 'the recipients of the charity should be brought up as much amongst other children as possible, and not to be taught to look upon themselves as recluses, or the inmates of an asylum, shut off from the rest of the world'.

87.   Tiviot Dale, c.1826.

88.   Tiviot Dale, looking up Lancashire Hill, c.1905.

89.   Pendlebury Hall viewed from Lancashire Hill.

90.   Pendlebury Hall.

From Lancashire Bridge to Mersey Square

At the turn of this century, the Mersey was completely open between these two points and, in order to walk from one to the other, it was necessary to use either the Underbanks and Chestergate to the south of the river or the road to the north, then known as Heaton Lane and now called Princes Street. This change of name was made in honour of the Prince of Wales, following his visit to Stockport in 1908 to open the Town Hall.

In 1936 an ambitious scheme was started to bridge 412 yards of the river with a new roadway, thereby improving traffic flow and giving better access to the mills and warehouses which lined its banks. The first Merseyway was opened on 1 April 1940 with little ceremony, the occasion overshadowed by the country's preoccupation with war.

Few of the industrial buildings survived the construction of the new Merseyway shopping precinct in the 1960s and only the southern end of Mersey Square remains intact.

91. Tram in Princes Street.

92. The river prior to the construction of Merseyway.

93. & 94. Construction of Merseyway, c.1939. The river was bridged between Lancashire Bridge and Mersey Square.

Mersey Square

Originally, this was an open area known as Carr Green, used by visiting funfairs as well for the recreation of the general public. In the 19th century Mersey Mill was built here, by the side of the river. With the coming of the tramcar, the factory was demolished to make way for a tram depot. On 31 January 1904 a second depot was opened on the site of the old gasworks on the corner of Heaton Lane and Wellington Road North (now a multi-storey car park).

Many will remember the *Touchstone Inn*, demolished to make room for Debenham's; some may also remember the fire station on the site now occupied by the main entrance to the shopping precinct. Built in 1902 and demolished in the 1960s, tragedy struck on 29 December 1926 when the fire engine 'Mary Dalziel' crashed through the parapet of Wellington Bridge and fell into the street below, killing Superintendent Howard Beckwith.

95. A view along Chestergate from Lower Carr Green (now Mersey Square) in 1895. This photograph was taken during the construction of a sewage tunnel to Heaton Mersey.

96. Sheep on Daw Bank. Wellington Bridge and Mersey Square are in the background.

97. Mersey Square, c.1934. On the left is the fire station and, next to it, the tram depot. In the foreground can be seen the bridge over the River Mersey.

98. Traffic in Mersey Square.

99. A view of Mersey Square from Daw Bank, *c.*1920.

100. Wellington Road South, *c*.1910. Heaton Lane is on the left.

Wellington Road

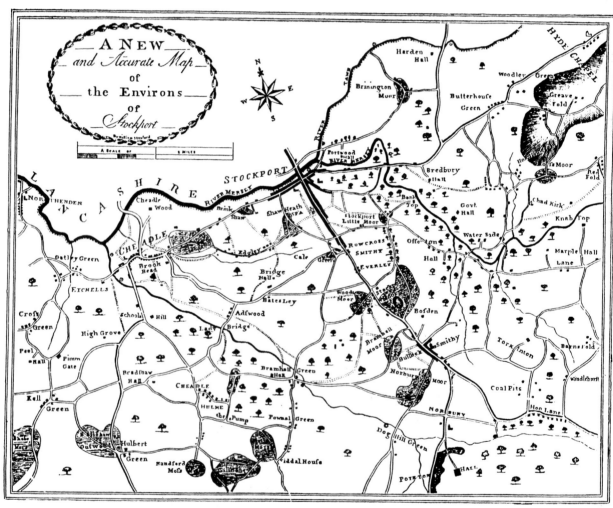

101.   A map of Stockport and the surrounding area, *c.*1800.

Stockport Railway Viaduct

The viaduct is surely Stockport's most famous landmark, crossing the Mersey valley 111 feet above the river and granting London-to-Manchester rail passengers a bird's eye view of the town. This mammoth structure is 6 ft. higher than the Menai Bridge, 1,786 ft. long, 53 ft. 4ins. wide, and has 22 main arches of 63 ft. span, as well as 4 arches of 22 ft. span. A comparison of the brickwork reveals that the eastern side is much older than the western side. The viaduct, which had been completed on 21 December 1840 after 21 months, was originally only 31 ft. wide, with one up and one down line. The first passenger train crossed here on 10 May 1842.

As rail travel increased, it was found necessary to widen the rail bridge to four lines, this work being completed in 1887. Disaster struck on 30 November 1948 when two trains crossing the viaduct crashed and five people were killed.

102.   Widening of the railway viaduct in 1887.

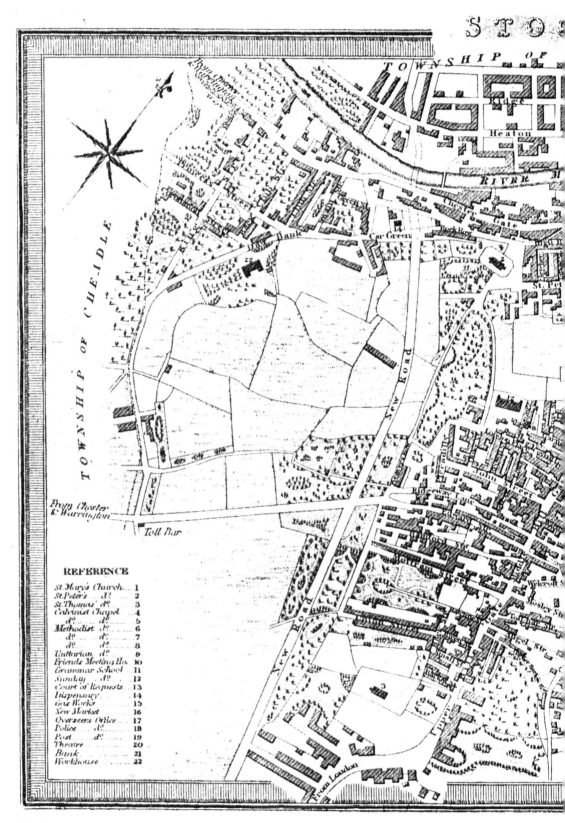

REFERENCE

St. Mary's Church.......1
St. Peter's   do.........2
St. Thomas'   do.........3
Calvinist Chapel.........4
    do.   do.........5
Methodist   do.........6
    do.   do.........7
    do.   do.........8
Unitarian   do.........9
Friends Meeting Ho..10
Grammar School.....11
Sunday   do......12
Court of Requests...13
Dispensary............14
Gas Works.............15
New Market...........16
Overseers Office.....17
Police   do........18
Post   do........19
Theatre..................20
Bank......................21
Workhouse.............22

103. A map of Stockport in 1824, before the coming of the railway. The New Road (Wellington Road) is clearly seen passing through fields and gardens.

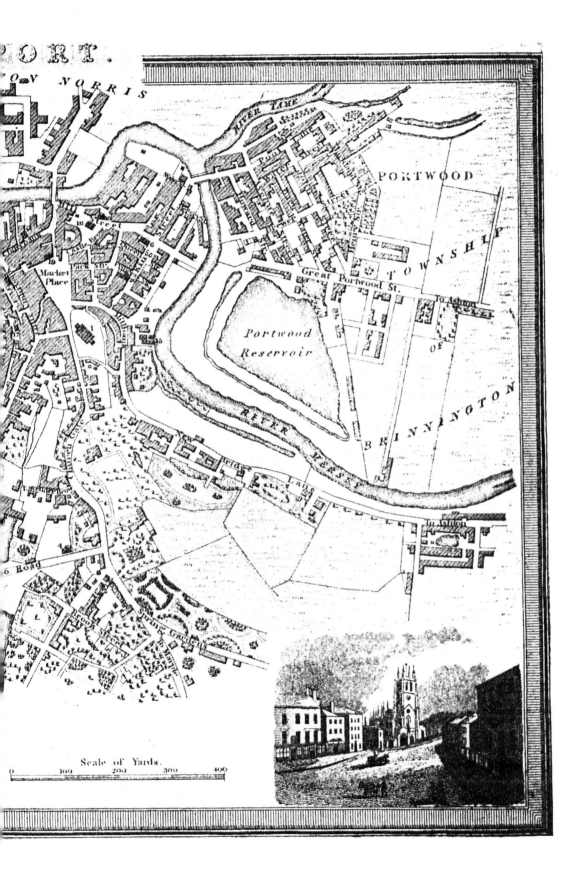

ORT.

TON NORRIS

RIVER TAME

PORTWOOD

TOWNSHIP

Pool Street

Great Portwood St.

To Ashton

OF

Portwood
Reservoir

BRINNINGTON

Market
Place

Park St.

RIVER MERSEY

Bridge Lane

To Ashton

Road

Brook Street

Spring Gardens

Scale of Yards.

0   100   200   300   400

104. Celebration to commemorate the placing of the last stone on one of the viaduct arches during widening, 1887.

105. Widening of the railway viaduct, *c.*1888. Notice the horse-drawn carts in the middle foreground.

106. A painting of Victorian Stockport. Brinksway is on the left.

107. The Mersey and railway viaduct.

108. The Mersey on its way to Liverpool.

Mechanics' Institute/Central Library

Stockport Central Library was opened on 14 October 1913, funds having been donated to the people of Stockport by the internationally renowned philanthropist Andrew Carnegie.

The site had previously been occupied by the Mechanics' Institute, constructed for the purpose of encouraging the study of the Arts and Sciences. Opened with great ceremony on 22 September 1862, the Institute contained a number of classrooms, a reception room, large library, reading room and a Great Hall with seating capacity for 1,000 people.

109. Stockport Mechanics' Institute, *c.*1880, now the site of Stockport Central Library.

110. Stockport Central Library.

National Schools/Town Hall

Stockport's most majestic edifice, the Town Hall, stands in a prominent position on Wellington Road South. Opened in July 1908 by the Prince (later to become George V) and Princess of Wales, Sir Alfred Bramwell Thomas's design was heavily influenced by the London churches of Sir Christopher Wren – as shown by his 'wedding-cake' tower which stands 130 ft. above the ground. Inside, the entrance hall is ornately decorated with Italian marble panelling and columns, whilst Sicilian marble has been used to construct a double staircase in the Renaissance style.

The National Schools which had once stood here was opened in 1827 to accommodate the 3,000 children who were being educated in the 'National Religion' (Anglican). Containing two very large school rooms each 104 ft. x 40 ft., this became the only church school in the town, replacing many smaller ones attached to individual churches.

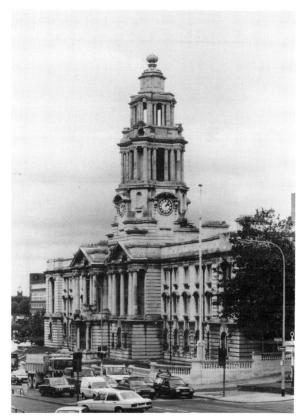

111. Stockport Town Hall viewed from the Art Gallery.

112. Stockport Town Hall. On its left stands Ebenezer chapel, whilst beyond Edward Street Mount Tabor chapel can be seen.

Mr. A. E. Ferns J.P., Deputy Mayor, Chairman of the Town Hall Committee.

Sir Brunwell Thomas, Architect.

Mrs. Ferns.

The Mayor and Mayoress.

Alderman Henry Bell, D.L. and Mrs. Bell.

Key presented to H.R.H. The Prince of Wales.

Master Henry Arthur Dalziel Ferns.

Master Geoffrey Thomas Bell.

113. Sir Brunwell Thomas, architect of the Town Hall, together with the Mayor, Deputy Mayor and their families.

114. The Town Hall under construction.

115. The Prince of Wales inspecting the Guard of Honour on Tiviot Dale Station Square, 7 July 1908.

116. The Prince and Princess of Wales, preceeded by the Mayor and Mayoress, entering the Town Hall.

117. Laying the Town Hall foundation stone by Alderman G. Atherton, Mayor, 15 October 1904.

118. Placing the top stone on the Town Hall by Alderman Bell, Mayor, 30 January 1907.

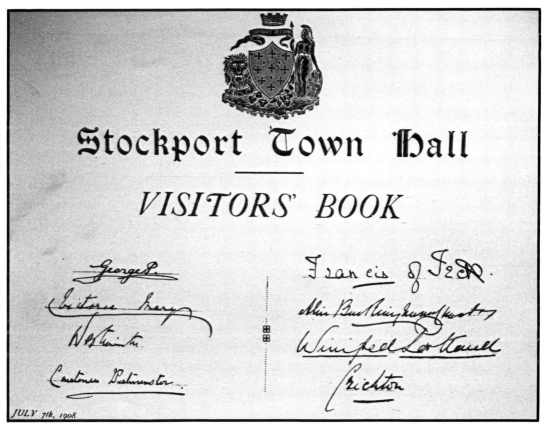

119. The first page in the visitors' book of Stockport Town Hall. The signatures are those of the Prince and Princess of Wales, the Duke and Duchess of Westminster, Prince Francis of Teck, the Duchess of Buckingham and Chandos, the Duchess of Portland, and Viscount Crichton.

120a. & b. Obverse and reverse of the medal struck to commemorate the opening of the Town Hall.

ICH DIEN

H.R.H. THE PRINCE OF WALES

H.R.H. THE PRINCESS OF WALES

121.   Frontispiece of the souvenir programme presented to the dignitaries.

James Briscall (1751-1814) and the Stockport Infirmary

The history of Stockport Infirmary can be traced back to 1774 when a young surgeon named James Briscall came to the town. Seeing the plight of the poor and needy of Stockport, he opened a consulting room in a thatched cottage in Churchgate – now the site of an inn of the same name. A short time later he moved, at his own expense, to a cottage in Grapes Steps, Hillgate, the most densely populated and poorest area in the town. He stayed here until 1792 when a public dispensary was opened in Millgate.

However, as the population increased with the growth of the cotton industry, it became evident that purpose-built premises were required. In 1797 the Dispensary and House of Recovery was opened at Cale Green, an area which at this time was only fields and gardens. James Briscall remained connected with this institution until his death; he was buried in the parish church.

122. A portrait of James Briscall.

In later years it again became necessary to find a larger site. Using land donated by Lady Vernon and with money generously given by benefactors, the foundation of Stockport Infirmary was laid. It was opened amidst great celebrations on 24-25 July 1833. The Doric-styled frontage appeared very much as it does today but without the south and north wings, these being added in 1871 and 1900 respectively.

123. Grapes Steps Cottages, Middle Hillgate, *c.*1901. It was here that James Briscall held his surgery.

124.   This view, *c*.1830, shows Stockport Infirmary on the left; the wings had not yet been added. On the right are the National Schools, now the site of the Town Hall.

125.   The Infirmary, *c*.1986.

Edward Street

Beyond the Town Hall lies Edward Street, occupied mainly by local government buildings. However, Joe Eaton, author and freeman of Stockport, recalls that in his childhood at the turn of the century there were at least three public houses and 26 shops in the street. Where Hollingdrakes Garage now stands, a windmill once ground corn for the lord of the manor. Demolished in 1857, it almost reached a premature end on 5 December 1822, when a fierce storm blew off the sails.

Mount Tabor chapel

All that remains of Mount Tabor chapel are four finely carved stone blocks in the little garden at the side of Edward Street. Built in the classical style by the Methodists to replace a smaller church, the foundation stone was laid on 25 October 1865. Completed at a cost in excess of £9,000, it was opened four years later. The chapel was able to accommodate 900 people. In order to enter the building, it was necessary to climb a massive flight of stairs which extended the width of the building and to pass through a Corinthian portico which consisted of four huge columns made from stone quarried at Darley Dale in Derbyshire. The columns were topped with capitals and when the building was demolished in 1969, these were preserved as a reminder of its magnificence.

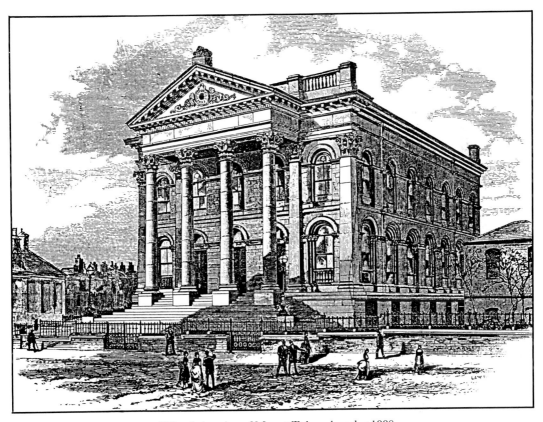

126.   A drawing of Mount Tabor chapel, *c.*1880.

War Memorial and Art Gallery/Grammar School

Across Wellington Road South stands a further example of the town's passion for neo-classical buildings – the War Memorial and Art Gallery, previously the home of Stockport Grammar School from 1832-1916. A temporary memorial to the soldiers of Stockport killed during the Great War of 1914-18 was unveiled here on 31 July 1921; the present memorial was unveiled on 15 October 1925 by H.R.H. Prince Henry.

127.   A drawing of Stockport Grammar School *c.*1888, before it moved to Davenport.

128.   Mount Tabor and the Technical College (*centre*), *c.*1920. Stockport Grammar School and Greek Street are on the right. The sign notifies the intention to build a war memorial here.

129.   The oldest surviving record of Stockport Grammar School pupils, April 1837.

130.   Pupils of the Greek Street Grammar School.

Technical School/Stockport College for Further Education

Towards the end of the 19th century, there was a general feeling that the resources of the Mechanics' Institute did not meet the needs of the town's industry. On 3 March 1887 a meeting of the Council was held at the Borough Court House in Vernon Street (the Town Hall was not built until 1908), where it was decided that Queen Victoria's Golden Jubilee would be celebrated with:

> The establishment in Stockport of a Technical and Art School in which to educate our industrial and commercial classes in the principles of the sciences and arts underlying their trades.

Part of the playing fields of the Grammar School were purchased and the foundation stone for the building was laid on 8 September 1888. Twelve months later, classes began under the headship of Robert John Brown. These included courses in spinning, weaving, hat making and dyeing.

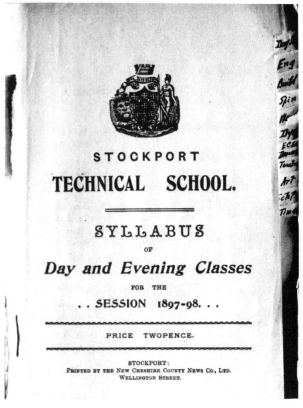

131. Robert John Brown, the first headmaster of Stockport Technical School, c.1900.

132. The syllabus for Stockport Technical School in 1897.

133.   The boys' class, *c.*1891.

134.   The girls' class, *c.*1891.

135. The Technical School teachers, *c*.1891.

136.   The spinning room, Stockport Technical School, *c*.1897.

137.   The carpentry class, *c*.1897.

138. The chemistry laboratory, *c*.1897.

139. Students being given a chemistry lesson, *c*.1897.

140.   Stockport Technical School, *c*.1890.

141.   During the First World War the main hall of the Technical School was used as a hospital, as can be seen in this 1917 photograph.

St Thomas's church

This church stands in St Thomas's Place, a few hundred yards beyond the remains of the Mount Tabor chapel. Erected on a site donated by Lord and Lady Warren-Bulkeley, construction commenced on 7 September 1822 and was completed at a cost of £15,000. The main entrance is via the western side and is distinctly Romanesque in style. The eastern side, however, has an entrancing Grecian portico, consisting of a pediment above six massive Ionic columns. The interior of the church is 100 ft. x 71½ ft. and, together with the spacious galleries which may be reached by stone staircases from the eastern entrance, will accommodate over 2,000 people.

142. St Thomas's church.

Hillgate

The large number of public houses which stand in isolation along this road are a clue to its history, for once this was the poorest and most densely populated area in Stockport, with whole families often living in single cellar rooms.

During the 19th century the town began to rely heavily on the cotton industry and the new machinery brought with it lower pay and higher unemployment. Hillgate became a hotbed of contention; in 1812 attempts were made to burn down Stockport's mills and two weavers were hung for their involvement in the troubles.

143. Mule and steam power, Middle Hillgate. This cartoon was a pun on the industry of the day, mules being those driven by steam power.

144. The corner of Edward Street and Middle Hillgate. Joseph Blackshaw, pawnbroker, is on the left. The *Old Admiral Inn* once stood here. On the right can be seen the archway into New Market. A market has never been held here as Stockport's charter does not allow a market to be held within five miles of the market place. It was therefore used as a coal and blacksmith's yard and as stables for tatters' horses and donkeys.

145. Bricklayers, *c.*1895. The wearing of hats was traditional and indicated a person's status.

146. The hat-forming shop, Christy & Co., 1937.

147. Hatting was one of Stockport's traditional industries. Taken in Christy's on Hillgate, this photograph shows Mr. Boardman finishing a bowler.

148. A drawing showing Stockport from Reddish in 1810.

149. Stockport from Reddish in 1885. A comparison with the drawing of 1810 gives an idea of its industrial growth in the 19th century.

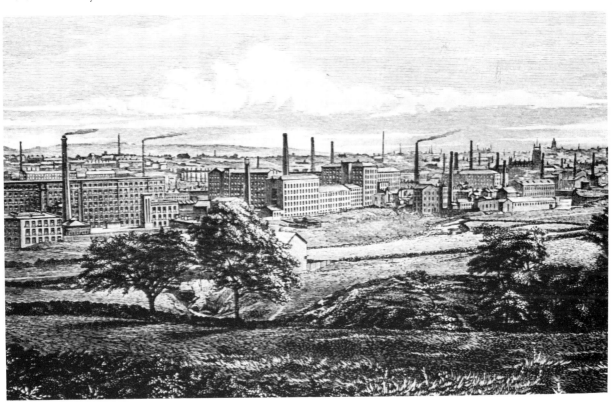

Samuel Oldknow

The rapidly developing technology of the 18th century brought about major changes in domestic life as the tradition of the family working unit began to disintegrate. The art of cloth making had always been a family affair carried out at home with children cleaning and preparing the fibres, women spinning (spinsters) and men weaving. Following James Hargreaves' invention of the Spinning Jenny in 1764, it became possible for a spinner to increase production by as much as 16-fold. Five years later, Richard Arkwright patented the Water Frame. This mechanical spinning machine required a constant supply of fast-flowing water and, as a result, it became necessary for spinners to work in purpose-built factories. In 1779 Samuel Crompton combined the roles of the water frame and the moveable carriage of the jenny to form the Spinning Mule. This invention was particularly suitable for spinning fine yarns and weft and was capable of achieving the same results as 3,000 hand spinners.

Samuel Oldknow was born in Anderton near Bolton on 5 October 1756. Having served an apprenticeship in Nottingham, he came to Stockport in 1785 and built the Hillgate Mill for the manufacture of muslin, using the newly invented Spinning Mule. Six years later he installed the first power steam engine in the town. Heginbotham records that 'such was the curiosity respecting the marvellous power of the steam engine at this time that the drivers of the London coaches, when passing this mill, slackened their speed in order to tell of the miraculous operations performed therein'.

Like many mill owners of his time, Samuel Oldknow used child apprentices in his mill. They were often obtained from orphanages and workhouses in London and Kent. The minimum age at which a child could legally be employed for a 14-hour working day in a mill was seven, although four-year-old apprentices were not unknown. Samuel Oldknow died on 18 September 1828 and was buried at Marple.

150. Samuel Oldknow's house, now part of Christy's Hat Works.

151. Mule spinning in Stockport, 1910.

152. Flax drying on Turncroft Lane, *c*.1920. Flax is used to produce linen.

The Blanketeers and the shooting of Constable Birch

The injustices of the Corn Laws brought about discontent and protest throughout Britain, especially in the manufacturing areas where economic depression added to the misery. On 10 October 1817 Bagguley, Drummond and Johnston, three notable opponents of the Corn Laws, spoke to a crowd which had assembled at Sandy Brow in Stockport. This so alarmed the authorities that they called on the Cheshire Yeomanry to assemble at the *Warren Bulkeley*, mounted and with pistols ready. Although the event passed peacefully, the Yeomanry were ordered to assemble each Friday at the inn for sword exercise.

On 10 March 1817 hundreds of Stockport people joined many thousands at a rally in St Peter's Field in Manchester. Many had walked long distances and so carried blankets and rugs to serve as beds on their journey. When the crowd refused to disperse, the Riot Act was read and over 200 ringleaders were arrested. 'The Blanketeers', as they subsequently became known, re-assembled and decided to march to London to protest. On reaching Lancashire Hill they were attacked by the Yeomanry and many people were severely injured. However, 180 managed to reach Macclesfield but were caught and returned to Stockport where they were locked in 'the castle'.

On 13 March, 21 of these Blanketeers were taken under escort to Chester, having been charged with 'treasonable and seditious practices'. Most were released without trial but the leaders Bagguley, Drummond and Johnston were sent to London for trial. Although they were released on bail on the condition that they behaved well, they continued to speak at protest meetings and were subsequently incarcerated in Chester prison. A song of the period included the verse:

> Bagguley, Drummond, and Johnston,
> In Chester Castle lies,
> For speaking of the Corn Laws,
> And opening of our eyes!

In protest over their unfair trial, the Reverend Joseph Harrison presided over a meeting in Stockport, at which over 4,500 signatures were collected. The petition was ignored. In July of the same year, Reverend Harrison and Sir Charles Wolseley were both arrested for making seditious speeches at a rally in the town. The arresting officer, William Birch of Spring Gardens, was shot by Jacob McGhinness, one of Harrison's supporters. McGhinness, a silk weaver of Edgeley, was tried and sentenced to death. Whilst awaiting his fate in prison he wrote his memoirs. William Birch survived and, since no bullet was found, it was often suggested that he had not in fact been shot. However, after his death on 26 May 1834, the *post mortem* examination discovered the bullet solidly embedded in his breast bone.

153.   The breastbone of Constable Birch.

D/14

JACOB M'GHINNESS;

OR,

A Memoir

OF

THE EXTRAORDINARY LIFE

AND

Wonderful Conversion

OF AN

INFIDEL, ATHEISTICAL REFORMER,

Who was executed at Chester, on April 15th, 1820, for shooting Mr. Birch of Stockport.

Written by Himself

WHILE UNDER THE SENTENCE OF DEATH.

TOGETHER WITH

THE REMARKS OF HIS BENEVOLENT VISITANT

MR. KEELING.

THE WHOLE

REVISED AND EDITED, WITH PRACTICAL NOTES AND REFLECTIONS,

BY THE

REV. J. HOLLIST,

MINISTER OF ST. JAMES'S, MANCHESTER.

SECOND EDITION.

Manchester:

Printed and Sold by J. GLEAVE, 196, Deansgate.

Sold also by the other Booksellers in Manchester; Hatchard and Seeley, London; Inkersley, Bradford; Hardcastle, Leeds; Wilson, Knaresborough; Spence and Burdikin, York; Clay and Lomax, Stockport; Seacomb, Chester; Wilson, Macclesfield; Rogerson, Blackburn; Haddock, Warrington; Kaye, Liverpool; Walker, Runcorn; C. and W. Thompson, Sheffield; Dunn, Nottingham; Ferraby Hull; and all other Booksellers.
1820.

PRICE SIXPENCE.

154. The memoirs of Jacob McGhinness, written while he was awaiting execution in 1820.

Gladstone Arms (formerly *Bishop Blaize*)

Cotton famine brought about by the American Civil War resulted in further economic depression and, by 1850, 69 mills had closed, 50,000 people were either unemployed or on half time and over 12,000 were receiving an income of less than 9¾d. per week. In Manchester the average life expectancy for members of the labouring class at this time was seventeen.

Friction between the immigrant Irish and the local English over employment resulted in ill-feeling and religious bigotry. Following a Catholic children's procession on 27 June 1852, a quarrel started at the *Bishop Blaize* between Irish and English labourers and a fight ensued. Both sides mustered reinforcements, but the police were able to separate the factions.

Several days later a group of Irishmen broke the windows of St Peter's School. This resulted in a riot where pokers, irons, sticks, stones, scythes and sickles were used as weapons. Having been driven back, the Irish were followed into their dwellings on Rock Row, with their beds, furniture and other articles being thrown into the street. The rioters proceeded to Edgeley where, now armed with crowbars, hatchets and pick-axes, the contents of the chapel of SS Philip and James were destroyed and attempts were made to burn the building down. The appearance of the military eventually contained the riots, although one man had been killed and 100 injured. Of the 10 Irishmen and 10 Englishmen sent for trial, one was transported for 15 years and the rest received between three months' and two years' imprisonment.

155. The *Bishop Blaize* public house, *c.*1852. It was here that the first disturbances in the Stockport riots took place.

156. The *Gladstone*, formerly the *Bishop Blaize*.

157. Rioters attacking SS Philip and James's Roman Catholic chapel at Edgeley, *c.*1852.

158. The attack on St Peter's Schools and Alderman Graham's house, *c.*1852.

Crowther Street

Opposite the *Gladstone Arms* is a row of isolated cobbled steps which were once lined with two- and three-storey houses. Fortunately, we have been left a reminder of life in this ancient backwater, for the artist L. S. Lowry came here in 1930 and his drawings reflect the hustle and bustle of life in Crowther Street and Hillgate.

159. Crowther Street in 1930, by L. S. Lowry.

160. Crowther Street as it appears today.

161. L. S. Lowry sketching Stockport Viaduct.

Waterloo Road

Connecting Hillgate with Churchgate, this thoroughfare was once a narrow lane with high hedges enclosing fields and gardens, the brook at the bottom of the valley being crossed by a bridge of planks. During the rebuilding of St Mary's parish church (1813-17), the opportunity was taken to widen Churchgate by removing 385 sq. yds. of the graveyard. The exhumed bodies were reburied, and gravestones and rubble from the old church were used in the construction of Waterloo Road. At this time, Canal Street (so named because a sluice of water ran alongside it to feed the small mills below) was a tree-lined avenue.

Further along Waterloo Road was Higher Carr Dam, a two-acre reservoir for the mills in the Carrs but used by the locals for skating in winter and boating in the summer. Unfortunately, on 2 December 1785 the dam gave way, causing great destruction of surrounding property.

John Dean lived in this area. He beat his pregnant wife to death with a heavy hand-brush and was subsequently hung at Chester. On 9 September 1790 his body was returned to Stockport where, accompanied by more than fifty horsemen and an immense crowd, it was carted in an iron cage to the gibbet at Great Moor near the junction of Dialstone Lane and Cherry Tree Lane. After several years his bones were buried and the irons sold to a neighbouring blacksmith. He was the last man to be hung on Stockport gibbet.

162.   The dam on Higher Carr, Waterloo Road.

163. The junction of Lower Hillgate, High Street and Wellington Street in 1907.

164. The same view today.

Robinson's Brewery

On 29 September 1838 William Robinson, a weaver and inn keeper of Bollington, purchased the *Unicorn Inn* on Lower Hillgate. Initially, the place was used for retailing a variety of ales and it was not until 1865, when his younger son Frederic entered the business, that the family began to brew their own beer. Their first customer was Mrs. Lamb who ran the *Bridge Inn* in nearby Chestergate. On 3 May 1876 Frederic purchased his first licensed house, *The Railway* at Marple Bridge, now known as *The Royal Scot*.

When Frederic died in 1890, he owned 12 licensed houses and since then the company has continued to flourish, their excellent brews being enjoyed throughout the North-West. In 1935 the *Unicorn Inn* was demolished, but the site is still part of Robinson's Unicorn Brewery on Hillgate.

165.   Frederic and Emma Robinson.

166. (below) Robinson's Brewery, Hillgate, in 1913. The building was demolished to widen the entrance for dray horses.

167. Robinson's Brewery, decorated to celebrate the coronation of George VI in May 1937.

168. Delivery vehicles from F. Robinson & Co. in 1922.

169. Coopers at work in Robinson's Brewery.

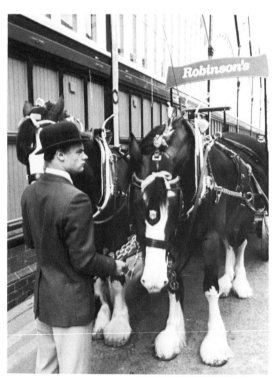

170. Robinson's dray horses in the market place.

Mealhouse Brow

Known earlier as Wynn-banke (winding or windy hill), the Brow obtained its current name from a mealhouse which stood at the top of the hill, in the market. Behind some of the houses which line the Brow stands a section of the medieval wall which once enclosed the town. Carts and pack-horses would use this steep lane and, on their descent, the horses were attached to the rear of the cart or coach to act as brakes, the leading horse wearing a bell to warn of their approach.

On 24 September 1860 a disaster occurred at the Brow when seven people were trampled to death following a firework display to celebrate the laying of the foundation stone of a tower in Vernon Park. The tower was never completed.

171.   Rostron Brow, one of the ancient tracks into the market place.

172.   Lower Hillgate, *c*.1910.

173.   View of Lower Hillgate.

174.   A business card of Messrs. Kay Bros. on Lower Hillgate. Rostron Brow can be seen on the left. Kay Bros. are the forerunners of Kay-Metzeler Ltd. of Bollington, polyurethane foam manufacturers.

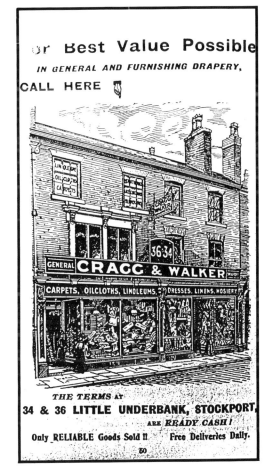

175.   Advertisement for Cragg & Walker, 34 & 36 Lower Hillgate.

176. Junction of Little Underbank and Mealhouse Brow. Petersgate Bridge can be seen in the distance.

The Cheshire Farmer

During George III's reign, Britain's opposition to America's fight for independence was very unpopular and a great deal of unrest was provoked by new taxes to raise money for the ventures.

On 27 November 1784, in protest at a levy on the use of saddle-horses, Jonathan Thatcher, a local farmer, rode to Stockport market on the back of a cow. The incident caused quite a sensation and a local artist drew a caricature, depicting the farmer on Little Underbank at the foot of Mealhouse Brow. The *Sun Inn* (later renamed the *Albion*) stands on the corner. The incident is also portrayed in the mural on the side of the British Home Stores building.

The mealhouse at the top of the Brow had two other functions. It housed the town dungeon and the Court Leet was also held there.

THE CHESHIRE FARMER'S POLICY, OR Pitt OUTWITTED.

Tax on Horses shall be void
For on my Cush I mean to ride

Let each like me strive to outwitt
And drown all Taxes in a PITT.

177. A contemporary drawing of Jonathan Thatcher riding his cow into Stockport, *c.*1784. Mealhouse Brow is in the centre.

Stockport Court Leet

The lord and lady of the manor of Stockport held a Court Leet twice a year, when the mayor and constables of the town would be appointed. They, in turn, would appoint tax collectors, food inspectors, weights and measures inspectors, dog muzzlers and the local beadle. Offenders against the law would be tried here by a steward, aided by a jury of between 12 and 23 townsfolk who had been residents of Stockport for a year and a day and were aged between 12 and 60 years.

The dual role of the building caused much mirth to onlookers. A writer in an early edition of *The Stockport Advertiser* wrote:

> Is it not a ludicrous spectacle to see the Mayor and Aldermen and gentry of Stockport marching in grand procession with a band of music and all the insignia of municipal office, to hold their Court and sit in Council in a dirty Mealhouse; all crowding pell mell into a poor unplastered room, hardly superior to the meanest stable in town, and all the assembly in danger of knocking their dignified heads against the ceiling, or metamorphosing their blue surtouts into the floury habiliments of a dusty miller?

By the 1840s the conflicting roles of the Court Leet and the Corporation regarding the governing of the town had become incompatible. In 1843 the frequent jealousies and disputes were ended when the manorial rights were purchased by the Corporation. The last meeting of the Court Leet was held on Thursday 21 October 1858.

178. Until 1870, constables were appointed by the Court Leet. This photograph shows a leather helmet dating from *c.*1820, which bears the Arms of Stockport.

The Dungeon

The dungeon was built of brick and stone, the entrance being an ancient nail-studded oak door fitted with a double-locked iron grating. The cell measured 12 ft. 9 ins. x 6 ft. 3 ins. and had a maximum headroom of six feet. The stocks were not the only form of punishment for minor offenders in Stockport; other punishments included:

The Brank or *Scold's Bridle*. This was mainly used for punishing females and consisted of an iron helmet with a metal plate designed to enter the mouth and thus curb the tongue. The Stockport brank had a two-inch plate at the end of which was a bulb from which projected eight iron barbs. A leather thong was also attached for dragging the offender through the market place.

The Ducking Stool. This was a chair attached to a long pole and mounted in such a manner that the seated offender could be swung over a pond and immersed in water. Used in Stockport until the middle of the 18th century, it is thought that the pool generally used for this purpose was at Cale Green.

179. An 1880 drawing of the scold's bridle used in Stockport.

The Whipping Post. Last used in 1820, the whipping post was a much-feared construction to which the offender was tied by the wrists, stripped to the waist and lashed with a heavy nine-tailed whip. Originally, the T-shaped post was fitted into a socket in the centre of the market place, but as visitors to the flogging disrupted normal market activity, the post and offender were transported by cart to a more convenient place.

The Pillory. Again situated in the market place, this degrading instrument of punishment consisted of a platform upon which was mounted a wooden frame with holes through which the offender put his head and hands. The onlookers would then throw all manner of offensive things at the unfortunate prisoner, including rotten eggs and dead cats.

Arts and Media

180.   March 1822. A facsimile of the first issue of the *Stockport Advertiser*, the town's longest running newspaper.

BY DESIRE OF
The Gentlemen of the Stockport

Armed Association.

THEATRE, STOCKPORT.

On FRIDAY, FEBRUARY 29th, 1805,

For the Second Time, the Last New Comedy of The

HONEY-MOON.

Now performing at the Theatre-Royal, Drury-Lane, with the highest marks of approbation and applause.

Duke of Aranza, (in love with, and afterwards the husband of, Juliana), Mr. DYER.
Count Montalban, (in love with Volante), Mr. LAMBERT.
Rolando, (rejected by Juliana, and pretending a general dislike to women), Mr. SEYMOUR.
Balthazar, (a Painter, father of Volante, Juliana, and Zamora), Mr. FROST.
Lampedo, (an Apothecary), Mr. DAVIS.
Campillo, (Steward to the Duke), Mr. PLATT.
Jaques, (Servant to the Duke, and sometimes assuming his Character), Mr. HAYES.

Juliana, } Daughters { Miss JOHNSON.
Volante, } of { Mrs. WAKEMAN.
Zamora, } Balthazar, { Mrs. QUANTRELL.
Hostess, Mrs. HENRY.
Masqueraders, Miss STORDY, &c.

End of Act 4th, incidental to the Piece,

A Pastoral Dance, by the Characters.

In the Course of the Evening, (by Desire)

A favorite Song, by Mrs. Creswell.

A COMIC SONG, BY MR. DAVIS.

A Dance, by Miss Stordy.

With the Musical Entertainment of

The Agreeable Surprise;

OR,

The LEARNED BUTLER.

Lingo, (the Learned Butler), Mr. DAVIS.
Sir Felix Friendly, Mr. HAYES.
Eugene, Mr. LAMBERT.
Compton, Mr. SPENCER.
John, Mr. QUANTRELL.
Chicane, Mr. FROST.
Cudden, Mr. POTTS. William, Mr. PLATT.
Cowslip (with all the original Songs), Mrs. CRESWELL.
Laura, Mrs. QUANTRELL.
Fringe, Mrs. HENRY.
Mrs. Cheshire, Mrs. WAKEMAN.

Doors to be opened at Six, and begin Seven o'Clock. Boxes, 3s.—Pit 2s.—Gal. 1s.

J. CLARKE, PRINTER.

THEATRE, STOCKPORT.

By Desire, & Positively the Last Night,

FOR THE BENEFIT OF THE

MESDAMES FERZI,

Who, in announcing their Benefit, presume to solicit a share of public favour; which, should they obtain, they will sensibly feel, and gratefully remember.

On FRIDAY, Jan. 26th, 1821.

The Entertainments will commence precisely at Seven o'Clock, with (for the first time, here) the Ascension and Descension of a Grand and Magnificent

BALLOON

designed, painted, and splendidly decorated, in exact imitation of the one in which MONSIEUR GARNERIN ascended from the Thuilleries in Paris, in honour of the ever-memorable VICTORY of WATERLOO.

During the Evolutions of this Grand Transparent Machine,

THE YOUNG AMERICAN

will, in the act of its Ascension and Descension from the Stage to the Gallery and back again, perpendicularly

Exhibit himself on his Head!

Keeping Equilibrium during the whole of this astonishing and ARDUOUS FEAT, which he has performed in ASTLEY'S Amphitheatre, London, with unbounded applause.

The Public are respectfully informed that, in consequence of the extensive preparation attending the Erection, &c. &c. it will commence the Evening's Performances

Immediately after will be performed the admired Comedy of THE

SPOIL'D CHILD.

Little Pickle, ... Miss HUGGINS Miss Pickle, ... Mrs. CLARKE
Old Pickle, ... Mr. SANDON Maria, ... Mrs. NORTHOUSE
Tagg, ... Mr. NORTHOUSE Margery, ... Mrs. E. HUGGINS
John, ... Mr. E. HUGGINS Susan, ... Mrs. GILBERT
Thomas, ... Mr. STANNARD

Immediately after which, Madame N. FERZI will perform her truly elegant Evolutions on the

SLACK WIRE,

and will, among a variety of NEW TRICKS, conclude her performances with Balancing

A PYRAMID OF FORTY LIGHTED CANDLES.

The YOUNG AMERICAN, who still continues to be received with unbounded applause, will perform his AERIAL TOURBILLIONS on the CORDE VOLANTE.

Madame S. FERZI will, on this occasion, particularly exert herself on the

Tight Rope:

In the course of her performances, she will introduce

A variety of unequalled Evolutions;

And will conclude her performance with the SIX DIVISIONS of the

BROAD SWORD EXERCISE!

never attempted by any other performer but herself.

The Mesdames FERZI will go through their fascinating Performances on the

TWO ROPES:

In the course of which, they will dance a New Pas de Deux, entitled "LE BERGERE DE GALLANT," as danced by them before the Allied Sovereigns, at the Grand Federal BURLINGTON HOUSE, given in honour of his Grace the DUKE of WELLINGTON.

A FAVOURITE SONG, ...by Mr. GILBERT.
A COMIC SONG, ...by Mr. E. HUGGINS.
A COMIC SONG, ...by Mr. NORTHOUSE.

To conclude with the musical Entertainment called

LOCK AND KEY.

Brummagem, ... Mr. SANDON
Cheerly, ... Mr. GILBERT Laura, ... Mrs. NORTHOUSE
Captain Vain, ... Mr. NORTHOUSE Fanny, ... Mrs. E. HUGGINS
Ralph, ... Mr. C. HUGGINS

Doors to be opened at Six, and the performance to commence at Seven o'Clock. Boxes, 3s. Pit, 2s. Gallery, 1s.—Half-price at half past Eight.

Tickets to be had of Mr. HUGGINS, at Mr. HAMPSON's, Little Underbank; of Mr. CLARKE, at Mrs. DUTTON's, Chestergate; and of Mr. LOMAX, Printer, where places for the Boxes may be taken.

181-4.   Four billposters for Stockport theatres.

THEATRE ROYAL
OPERA & HOUSE
St. Peter's Sq.

Proprietors   (Also Proprietors, Theatre Royal, Ashton-u-Lyne)   Messrs. REVILL, Voeweod.
Acting Manager   JOHN REVILL   Business Manager and Secretary   CHARLES REVILL.
TELEPHONE 2156.

MONDAY, SEPT. 6th, for 6 Nights & 1 Matinee
MATINEE: WEDNESDAY, AT 2-30
CONTINUOUS MONDAY TO FRIDAY

6-15 | TWICE NIGHTLY | 8-15

LET'S ALL GO-
TO SEE

BILLY RUSSELL

"ON BEHALF OF THE WORKING CLASSES"
The Famous Star Comedian from the Palace, Manchester

DOROTHY **LIVESEY**	The 100% Personality Girl **BEBE NORMA**	Songs and Comedy **ROBB & DOBB**
Lancashire's Own Lady Ventriloquist With JACKIE & GINGER	Dancing Wizard of the Xylophone	T'other Mother Riley

JACK E. **RAYMOND**	MAX RIVERS' **TWO MAXETTES**
The Happidrome and Worker's Playtime Favourite Laughing the Blues Away	A Novelty in the Wonders Dancing

3 ASTOUNDERZ 3
Something Astounding in the Air

The "Ace" of Shadowgraphists
EDWARD VICTOR
Royal Command   "Hand Made" Humour

"LET'S ALL GO—TO A MUSIC HALL."

Fully Licensed Refreshment Lounges are open in each part of the Theatre

Dress Circle and Orchestra Stalls	Upper Circle	Pit Stalls	Balcony	Pit	Gallery
2/6	**1/9**	**1/9**	**1/-**	**9D**	**6D**
(Including Tax) No Extra Charge for Booking Private Boxes: Single Seats 3/6	(Including Tax) Reserved 2/6	(Including Tax) Reserved 2/6	(Including Tax)	(Including Tax)	(Including Tax)

Under the Patronage of His Worship the Mayor of Stockport.

Two Fine Concerts

The Proceeds, in equal proportions, in aid of the Stockport Infirmary and
St. Dunstan's Hostel for Soldiers and Sailors Blinded in the War

Stockport Choral and Orchestral Society
29th SEASON.

SECOND GRAND

CONCERT

MISCELLANEOUS : : (CHIEFLY ORCHESTRAL)

In the CENTENARY HALL, on
MONDAY, MARCH 7th, 1921

BAND (MOSTLY HALLE PLAYERS)
and **CHORUS**
... of 170 ...

Accompanist:—
Mr. ERNEST COOKSON.
Conductor:—
Mr. G. H. BROOME.

Doors open at 7 o'clock.
Concert 7·30.

PRINCIPAL VOCALISTS:

Miss LAURA EVANS-WILLIAMS.

TICKETS :
2/8 & 1/9, NUMBERED RESERVED;
1/- UNRESERVED.
Including Tax.

The Plan may be seen and Seats booked
at Messrs. Nield & Sons, Underbank.

Tickets may be had from Messrs. Nield &
Sons ; Madame Redfern-Williams' Successors ;
Messrs. White, 47, Wellington Road South ;
Beardsell Bros., 36, Castle Street ; J. Rothwell,
1, Hall Street ; or members of the Society.

Miss Laura EVANS-WILLIAMS
Of London.   THE BRILLIANT WELSH SOPRANO.

Mr. Charles R. BRIERLEY
BASS

Bibliography

Aiken, J., *A description of the country from thirty to fourty miles around Manchester*, 1795

Astle, W. (ed.), *History of Stockport*, 1922

Bird, D., *500 years of Stockport Grammar School*, 1987

Christie-Miller, J. (ed.), *Stockport and the Stockport Advertiser – A History*, 1972

Dictionary of National Biography

Earwaker, J. P., *East Cheshire Past and Present* (vols. 1 & 2), 1877

Eaton, J., *Hillgate*

Frederic Robinson Ltd., *A look inside the Brewery*

Heginbotham, H., *Stockport Ancient and Modern* (vols. 1 & 2), 1892

Hooley, J., *Old Taverns, Inns and Public Houses in Stockport*, 1978

Stockport College for Further Education, *Opening of Phase 2 also to commemorate 75th Anniversary*, 1964

Stockport Corporation, *Official Guide and Industrial Handbook* (1972-3 edition)

Stockport Grammar School, *Four Hundred and Fiftieth Anniversary*, 1937

Stockport Museum Education Service, *From the Ground Upwards*.